Things That Should Be in a Poem

In memory of my precious father, Gordon,
who always encouraged me to find the right words.

Published by TROIKA

First published 2022

Troika Books Ltd
Well House, Green Lane, Ardleigh CO7 7PD
www.troikabooks.com

Text copyright © Coral Rumble 2022
Illustrations copyright © Shih-Yu Lin 2022

The moral rights of the author
and illustrator have been asserted

All rights reserved

A CIP catalogue record for this book
is available from the British Library

ISBN 978-1-912745-20-3

1 3 5 7 9 10 8 6 4 2

Printed in Dubai by Oriental Press

Things That Should Be in a Poem

Coral Rumble

Illustrated by Shih-Yu Lin

troika

Contents

Things that Should be in a Poem	6
Down my Street	7
Ooowwww!	8
Corner Shop	10
Spy-Lady	12
Uh-Oh!	13
Monster	14
Grandad's Shed	16
Grandad's Boat	17
Feeding Ducks	18
Paddle-Waddle Ducks	20
My Name	22
Park Game	23
Dragon in a Shoe	24
Tidal Wave!	25
Dinosaur Ball	26
Sleepover	28
There's a Tiger Behind You	29
Amelia's Wish	30
Questions	32
Atchooooo!	34
The Pet Shop	36
Dry Dog	38
Charlie	39
Rabbit Rhythms	40
Cats Can	42
Cat on the Table	44

The Farmyard Cat	45
Farmyard Puddle	46
Frozen Puddles	47
At the Seaside	48
Pinch a Pod	49
Ten Jolly Pirates	50
Never Let a Worm	52
Magic Coat	54
Magic String	55
Hiding	56
Secrets	57
Daisy Life	59
Old Brown Bear	60
Brick on Brick	62
Tattered	63
Sled	64
Helter-Skelter Ride	66
I've Got a New Bike	67
Unicorn Uniform	68
Playtime Skipping	70
Bright	71
Big Boys	72
Mustafa's Jumper	74
Friday Feeling	75
Code	76
Invitations	77
Ting!	78

THINGS THAT SHOULD BE IN A POEM

The sleep in my eyes,
The wax in my ears,
The salt on my cheek
From stray night-time tears,

    The squeeze of my jumper,
    The swish of my hair,
    The crack in my curtain,
    The dust in the air,

        My skip on the pavement,
        My jump from the wall,
        The gathering treasure
        As large conkers fall,

The squelch of my boots,
The mud in their grooves,
The wobble of puddles
Before they go smooth,

A weekend of time,
A wide space to play,
I think I'll collect
A poem today.

DOWN MY STREET

Listen to the beat of the rushing feet
Of the people who live down my street.

    Down my street the children run,
    They kick a ball, have lots of fun,
    They skip and skate, they hide and seek,
    They sometimes laugh and sometimes SHRIEK!

Listen to the beat of the rushing feet
Of the people who live down my street.

    Down my street the women race,
    They zoom like rockets up in space,
    Hurry to school, hurry to the shops,
    Hurry to work, they never ever stop.

Listen to the beat of the rushing feet
Of the people who live down my street.

    Down my street the hurried men rush,
    They swing their arms, their faces flush,
    They check their watches on their way,
    Off to work for a busy day.

    Listen to the beat of the rushing feet
    Of the people who live down my street.

Howl, howl, howl,
As his lips make an 'O'
The shrill notes climb
As the decibels flow.

Howl, howl, howl,
His soprano voice goes on,
In operatic pitches
He sings his lonely song.

CORNER SHOP

Everyone stops at the corner shop,
The corner shop is the place to pop.
Whether it's cold, or whether it's hot,
My favourite place is the corner shop.

You can buy some bread
Or a plastic sled,
A morning paper
And sweets for later,

You can buy some glue
To fix your shoe,
A small steak pie
Or a trap for a fly,

You can buy a snack
And bin liner sacks
A colouring book,
A pack of hooks,

You can buy an apple,
Some fishing tackle,
A bottle of bleach,
A spade for the beach,

You can buy bags of logs
And food for your dog,
Some straw for a hutch
That's prickly to touch,

You can buy some soap,
Some string, and a rope,
A toy that is cheap
That won't last a week.

Everyone stops at the corner shop,
The corner shop is the place to pop.
Whether it's cold, or whether it's hot,
My favourite place is the corner shop.

SPY-LADY

There's a lady down our street
Who sits upon a seat
And watches all the people walking by.

    She sits in the fresh air,
    And turns her head to stare
    At neighbours she can't quite identify.

My best friend, Zephaniah,
Who is sharper than a spire,
Says he thinks that she is probably a spy.

    She always wears dark glasses,
    Follows everyone who passes
    And zooms in closely with her x-ray eyes.

We think she's on a mission,
Well, that is our suspicion,
So asking her some questions isn't wise.

    We just look the other way,
    When we go out to play,
    And leave her to collude with MI5.

UH-OH!

I'm stuck behind the sofa,
Mum doesn't know I'm here,
I'm supposed to be upstairs in bed
When dinner guests appear.

    I stayed to see the end
    Of a programme about sheep -
    It wasn't very interesting
    And hasn't made me sleep.

        I'm bound to be discovered soon,
        There's no other place to flee,
        Dad's walking up the stairs
        To say goodnight to me!

MONSTER

When I turn out the light
There's one thing that I dread,
And that is the monster
Who hides under my bed.

I've never heard him whimper,
I've never heard him roar,
I've never heard him growl
If I've stepped on his paw.

I've never felt his fur,
I've never touched his tail;
The thought of feeling his great jaws
Makes me go quite pale.

I've never smelt his scent
Or unmentionable pongs;
I've never smelt his poisonous breath,
Though I'm sure it must be strong.

I've never seen his eyes,
I've never seen his teeth,
But when I jump into my bed
I know he's underneath!

GRANDAD'S SHED

In Grandad's shed
Are tools that bang,
Nails that shine
And tins that clang.

In Grandad's shed
Are drills that hum,
A mug of tea,
Some biscuit crumbs.

In Grandad's shed
Are a spade and fork,
Some sacks of seed
And a bottle cork.

In Grandad's shed
Are balls of string
And boxes full
Of secret things.

In Grandad's shed
Are dusty boots,
Some broken things,
A horn that toots.

In Grandad's shed
Is his old, old bike,
I can sit on the saddle
Whenever I like.

In Grandad's shed
We stay awhile,
And talk and talk
And smile and smile.

GRANDAD'S BOAT

My grandad really likes to float
Up and down in his rowing boat.
He likes to row far out to sea
And sometimes he takes Mac and me.

And when he does take Mac and me,
He helps us catch fish for our tea.
And sometimes grandad lets me row
Across the waves, to and fro.

The seagulls squawk and make Mac bark,
The sun sinks low, the shore looks dark,
And then my grandad takes the oars
And rows us safely home once more.

FEEDING DUCKS WITH GRANDMA

When Grandma takes us to the park
Where the tree roots stretch and spread,
She says, before we have some fun,
The ducks must all be fed.

And when the ducks have all been fed,
Too full to flap their wings,
Then Grandma races really fast
And beats us to the swings.

PADDLE-WADDLE DUCKS

Paddle-waddle ducks skate
The dimpled, dappled river;
In and out of willow fringe,
Making tall reeds quiver.

Paddle-waddle ducks glide,
Ripples part and fade;
Up and under bobbing heads
Shine emerald and jade.

Orange flippers scoop beneath,
Yellow bills snap tight,
Wriggling tails and jerking heads
Spin and dart and fight.

Through daisy spots of froth
Ducks and drakes coast free;
Sudden wings lift up to bank
And roots of drooping trees,

Where paddle-waddle ducks
Close fine-weave feathers tight,
Shake water droplets from wing tips
And settle for the night.

MY NAME

Grandma says she knows my name
(And my picture's in her photo frame)
Sometimes my name is just mislaid
Like glasses, pens, or hearing aid.

>Sometimes, she searches for a while,
>Touches my lips, traces my smile,
>Then tells a tale I've heard before
>About a party dress she wore.

Sometimes she thinks I'm someone else,
Dad says, 'Now, don't upset yourself',
And in her eyes I see the spaces
She tries to fill with familiar faces.

>Her memories have gathered dust,
>She doesn't quite know who to trust,
>Some days she stares, some days she cries,
>And when she does, I wipe her eyes.

Grandma says she knows my name,
Just not at the moment when I came
To see her, but she hasn't lied,
I know my name is locked inside.

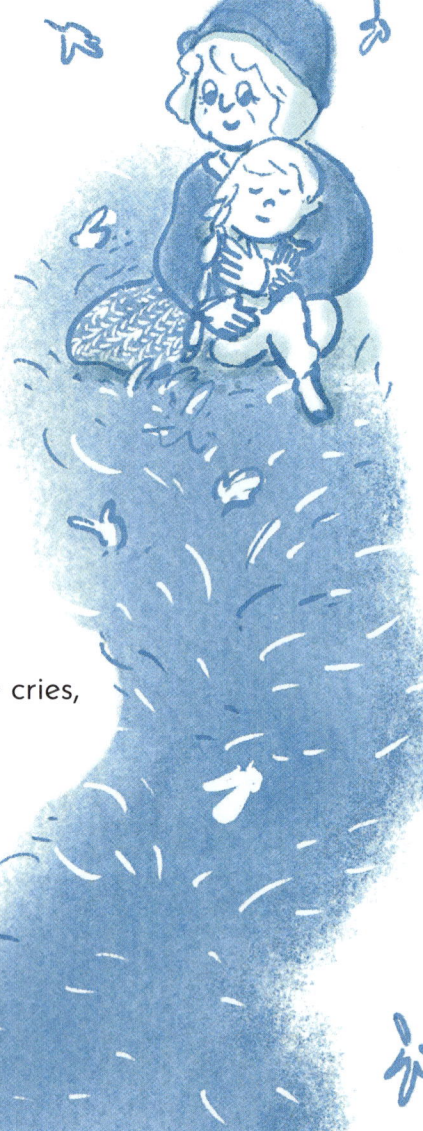

PARK GAME

    My brother races up the wing –
    He scores, they roar
    And shout and sing –
    But they won't let me play.

Ben begins a new attack
With pace to chase
Defenders back –
But they won't let me play.

    The others play with heart and soul;
    They pass with class
    Another goal! –
    But they won't let me play.

        Later on, my dad comes out,
        They win, he grins,
        I stare and pout –
        'Cause they didn't let me play.

DRAGON IN A SHOE

Jasper wondered who had put a dragon in his shoe,
It was tiny, it was scaly, it was green.
It puffed out little flames, so perhaps it wasn't tame,
It was quite the smallest dragon ever seen!

    Jasper wondered what to do about the dragon in his shoe;
    It was nearly time for school, he would be late,
    So he popped it in a box, the one he always locks,
    Left and ran, with speed, to the school gates.

Jasper's day was fun, although he worried for his mum
As she didn't know a dragon was upstairs;
If she opened up the box, the one he always locks,
She was sure to see the dragon and get scared.

    School ended and, quite soon, he was back inside his room
    To see another unexpected sight;
    There inside his trainer, nothing could be plainer,
    Was a tiny, shiny, armour-wearing knight!

The knight gave a little cough, as he took his helmet off,
And said, 'I've lost a dragon; help me look.
I've been chasing it for ages through your storybook pages,
Now we've crashed through the back cover of the book!'

    'The book under my bed? The one I haven't read?'
    Asked Jasper, as he closed his bedroom door.
    'That's right,' replied the knight, 'you should read about our fight;
    I win, and save a princess from his jaws!'

So Jasper let the dragon out, and the knight began to shout
As he chased the dragon back inside the pages,
Then Jasper lay and read, the book under his bed,
The one that had been lying there for ages.

TIDAL WAVE!

'There's a dinosaur in the swimming pool!'
Said the man at the Leisure Centre,
'There's a dinosaur in the swimming pool!'

And just then, the water came splashing,
And everyone was dashing,
As the water came gushing
The lifeguards were all rushing,
And the floats were bobbing by
While all the babies had a cry,
And the fountain stopped its spouting
And the mummies were all shouting,
And bats and balls and rackets
Were all awash in minutes,
And the lady from the shop
Floated by in quite a strop,
And the ladies from the sauna
Floated quickly round the corner,
While the large men from the gym
Dropped their weights so they could swim.

'It's okay now, he's gone to get changed,'
Said the man at the Leisure Centre,
'It's okay now, he's gone to get changed.'

PHEW, WHAT A RELIEF!

DINOSAUR BALL

Stamp your feet
And clap your hands,
Dance to the beat
Of the dinosaur band.

Swish your tail
Snap your jaws,
Nod your head
And tap your claws.

Wobble your belly,
Wiggle your nose,
Twirl around
On your dinosaur toes.

Stand in line,
Everyone jump,
Bump your bottoms
With a great big **THUMP**.

Dance and dance
'Til the night is done,
At the dinosaur ball
You'll have such fun!

SLEEPOVER

The whales are having a sleepover,
They'll giggle and wriggle all night,
They'll watch 'The Little Mermaid'
And have jellyfish pillow fights.
They'll experiment with make up
And polish their pectoral fins,
They'll have blowhole competitions
(The highest to spurt will win)
They'll tell jokes and laugh very loudly
Then lay down their tired whale heads,
Squeeze into their seaweed sleeping bags
And shuffle along the seabed.

'THERE'S A TIGER BEHIND YOU!'

If I tell my little sister,
'There's a tiger behind you!'
She cries
And I get into trouble.
And Mum says things like:
'Don't be so horrible!
How would you like it?
Remember she's only small.
She'll have bad dreams now.'
(And I suppose, if you're a grown up,
You'll understand her point.)
But if you had a little sister who:
Broke your remote-control car,
Pushed over your Lego model,
Scribbled on your best poster
And got far more cuddles than you,
You'd be tempted to tell her,
'There's a tiger behind you!'

AMELIA'S WISH

Amelia Belle has a tiger,
Quite an unusual pet,
And everyone goes very quiet
When she takes him along to the vet.

He likes to climb trees in the garden,
And walks on the fence like a cat,
He likes to curl up by the fire
On a big, fluffy, tiger-size mat.

Amelia Belle has a tiger
With eyes that glow like a flame,
He walks next to her on the pavement
And comes when she calls out his name.

One day, way back in October,
He followed her home from the zoo,
And now he's grown used to Amelia
And the things that her family do.

Amelia Belle has a tiger,
Which is better, by far, than a fish;
It just goes to show, on your birthday,
It's always worth making a wish.

QUESTIONS
(THE DAY AFTER A ZOO VISIT)

Teacher, teacher, tell me please
Why giraffes have knobbly knees,
And why their necks stretch to the sky
So that their heads end up so high?
And why their picture-puzzle backs
Are too far from their feet to scratch,
And why their legs are stiff and thin,
And why I've never seen one grin?
I've got some other questions too,
About the creatures in the zoo,
The questions rushed at me in bed,
I've got them written in my head.

And when you feel his sneeze
It will make you stop and freeze
As it rushes past your knees.

There is no stronger breeze
That travels through the trees,
ATCHOOOOO! Than an elephant's big sneeze.

A sniff and mighty wheeze
Always warns and guarantees
That an elephant will sneeze.

THE PET SHOP

In the corner of a pet shop,
In the shadows, fast asleep,
Is a tiny, weenie dragon,
You could take him home for keeps.

Behind the pet shop counter,
Is a lazy kangaroo
Snoozing through the afternoon,
He could bounce home with you.

Underneath a rabbit hutch,
Is a friendly crocodile,
He's waiting for an owner
Who will love him for his smile.

Inside a dusty cupboard
You can hear the quiet crying
Of a shy rhinoceros,
Who would like someone to buy him.

For this pet shop is quite different,
You're sure of a surprise,
Push open wide the creaky door,
You won't believe your eyes!

DRY DOG

Dry dog
On a log,
Sees a puddle
In the middle
Of a field.

Dry dog
Steps in bog,
Paws sink down,
Doggy frown,
Splash, whine, panic!

Dry dog
Jumps from log,
Tiptoes by,
Nose to sky,
Sniffing hard.

Dry dog
Slides in bog,
Eyeballs frog,
Soggy dog...
Back on log.

CHARLIE

Charlie isn't well today,
He's got no energy to play,
He's lying on the sofa, still,
There's no mistake, he's feeling ill.

    Yesterday he seemed okay,
    Acting in his normal way,
    But this morning he won't eat,
    His nose is hot, so are his feet.

        So, for today I'll stroke his head,
        Do everything the vet has said,
        I'll take him to my cosy den
        Until he wags his tail again.

RABBIT RHYTHMS

Crunch, crunch, crunch,
Go the teeth of our rabbit,
He's such a noisy eater
With a loud, chomping habit.

Rustle, rustle, rustle,
Goes the paper and the straw,
As he scratches at the walls,
As he nibbles at the door.

Thump, thump, thump,
Go his noisy drumming feet,
Banging out a rhythm
'Til you feel his rabbit beat.

CATS CAN

Cats can s t r e t c h

And cats can c u r l

Cats can p o u n c e

And t w i r l and t w i r l

Cats can
S
i
t

And cats can laze zzZ

And PuRR into A sleepy haze.

CAT ON THE TABLE

Cat on the table
Is more than able
To take a look
At what Dad cooks.

Cat on the table
Is more than able
To yowl for a bite
Of food in his sight.

Cat on the table
Is more than able
To stretch a claw
To swipe a paw.

Cat on the table
Is more than able
To pounce from behind
On bacon rind.

Cat on the table
Is more than able
With razor sharp teeth
And tricks of a thief.

THE FARMYARD CAT

Blink goes the farmyard cat,
As he searches round for mouse or rat,
As he darts his head and lifts his tail
And tip-toes out his hunter's trail.

Twitch go his ears and tiny nose,
As he darts around on nimble toes,
As he crouches low then, unannounced,
Zooms like an arrow in a perfect pounce.

FARMYARD PUDDLE

I'm a muddy, muddy puddle,
I can cause a lot of trouble
For a child who likes to get a little damp,
I love to feel the dashing,
The jumping and the splashing,
I love to fire splodges as they stamp.

        My tummy's brown and slushy,
        I am oozy, soft and mushy,
        I like to bubble up and throw some goo,
        So if you haven't got your wellies
        Go home and watch the telly,
        'Cause a farmyard puddle's not the place for you.

FROZEN PUDDLES

Frozen puddles make me struggle,
Set my arms and legs a muddle;
Slipping, sliding, smoothly gliding,
Wish I had a sleigh to ride in!

Crack the surface, press the ice
With your wellie, once or twice;
Underneath the water bubbles,
Laughing at our tripping troubles.

AT THE SEASIDE

We'll have a splish time, a splash time
A watch-the-tall-waves-crash time,
At the seaside.

We'll have a salty-sandy-hand time
A hear-the-big-loud-band time,
At the seaside.

We'll have a slippery-seaweed-smell time
A find-a-shiny-shell time,
At the seaside.

And we'll have a wave-goodbye-to-the-bay time
A wish-that-we-could-stay time
A hip-hip-hip-hooray time,
For the seaside.

PINCH A POD

Slimy seaweed,
(Slippery grip)
Slithering under
Finger tips.
Hold on tight,
Enjoy the ride,
Satisfaction
Multiplied.
Pinch a pod
And hear the SNAP!
Nature's gift
Of bubble wrap.

TEN JOLLY PIRATES

Ten jolly pirates
Splashing in a puddle,
Under big umbrellas
In a pirate huddle.

Ten jolly pirates
Wobbling their bellies,
Singing a sea shanty
In their pirate wellies.

Ten jolly pirates
Going splish and splat,
Catching tiny raindrops
In their crossbones hats.

Ten jolly pirates
Dancing on a plank,
Shivering their timbers
And getting very damp.

Ten jolly pirates
See the sun break through,
Then sail into the distance
To do what pirates do.

NEVER LET A WORM WRIGGLE DOWN YOUR WELLIE

Never let a worm
Wriggle down your wellie,
It will tickle round your toes
As it wiggles on its belly.
It will curl around your ankle,
It will snuggle in your sock
It will jiggle, loop and twist,
So get ready for a shock!
It will search around your heel,
You will feel its wormy wiggle,
It will stretch up to your shin,
It will make you smile and giggle.
No, never let a worm
Wriggle down your wellie,
It will squiggle, it will squirm
And your knees will turn to jelly.

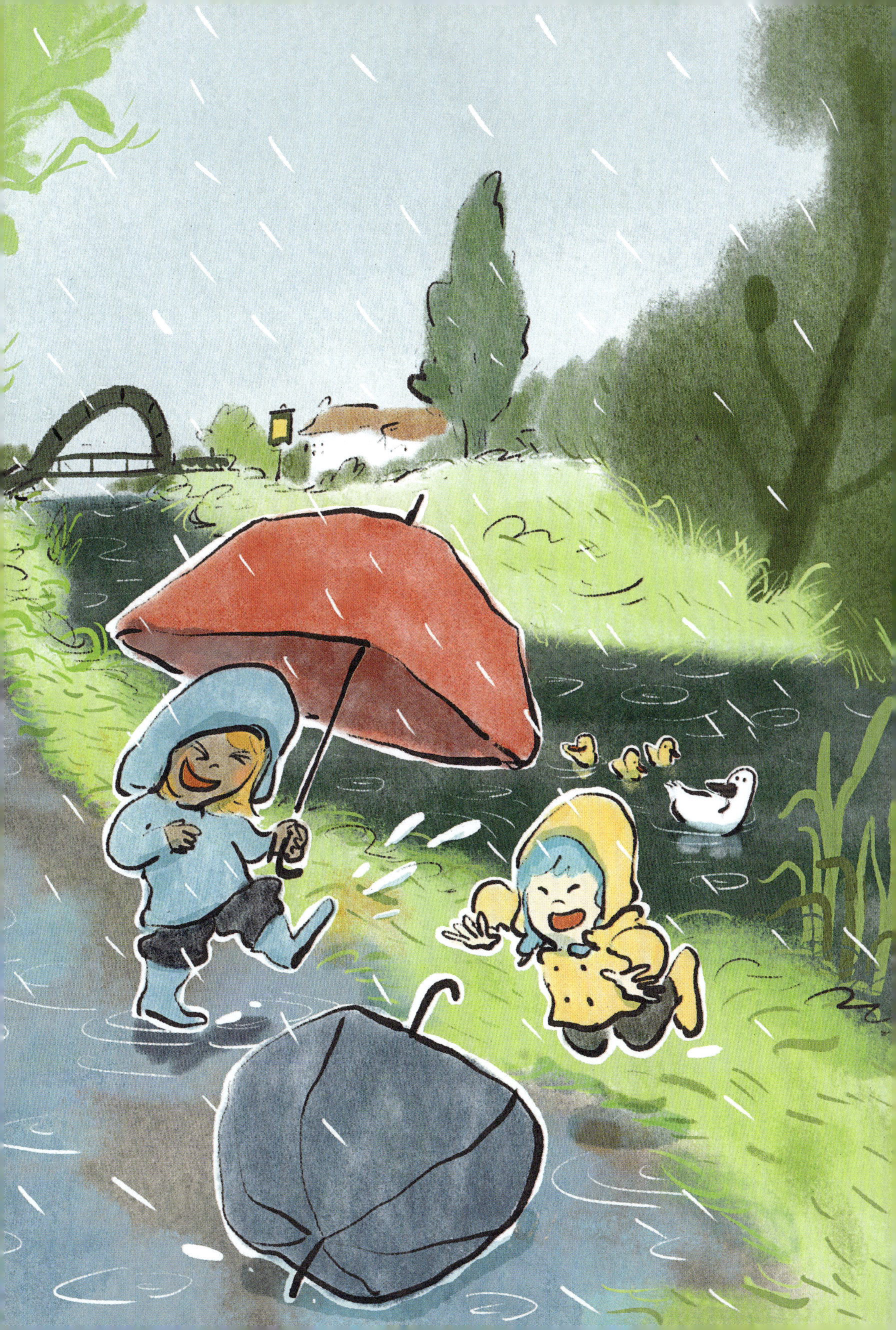

MAGIC COAT

If I had a magic coat
That made me very clever,
I'd wear it everywhere I went,
In every kind of weather.

    If I had a magic coat
    That made me fly up high,
    I'd wear it everywhere I went
    And travel through the sky.

        If I had a magic coat
        That made my legs run fast,
        I'd wear it everywhere I went
        And never more come last.

            If I had a magic coat
            I would feel so free,
            Doing things I just can't do
            When I am only me.

MAGIC STRING

I saw a kite above a field,
It climbed and flapped and fell,
A little boy held in his hand
Some string, which I could tell
Could make the kite do special tricks,
And twist and turn and loop the loop;
Jump autumn clouds and ride the wind,
And dive into an eagle swoop,
Until the wind moved on from there
And left the sky ice-cold and bare.

HIDING

Behind this tree
You can't see me,
I've made myself thin
So I can fit in.

I'm as still as a photograph,
As quiet as a blink,
I won't sniff or laugh,
Just quietly think.

Behind this tree
You can't see me,
I've made myself thin
So I can fit in.

SECRETS

I love secrets when they belong to me,
When all my friends crowd round
And whisper quietly.

I love secrets when they belong to friends
Who say that they can't share them,
But tell me in the end.

I love secrets when they belong to Mum,
They twinkle brightly in her eyes
And promise me some fun.

I love secrets when they belong to Dad,
Because he teases me with clues
And nearly drives me mad.

But I hate secrets when they snigger and they lie,
When they belong to someone else
Who wants to make me cry.

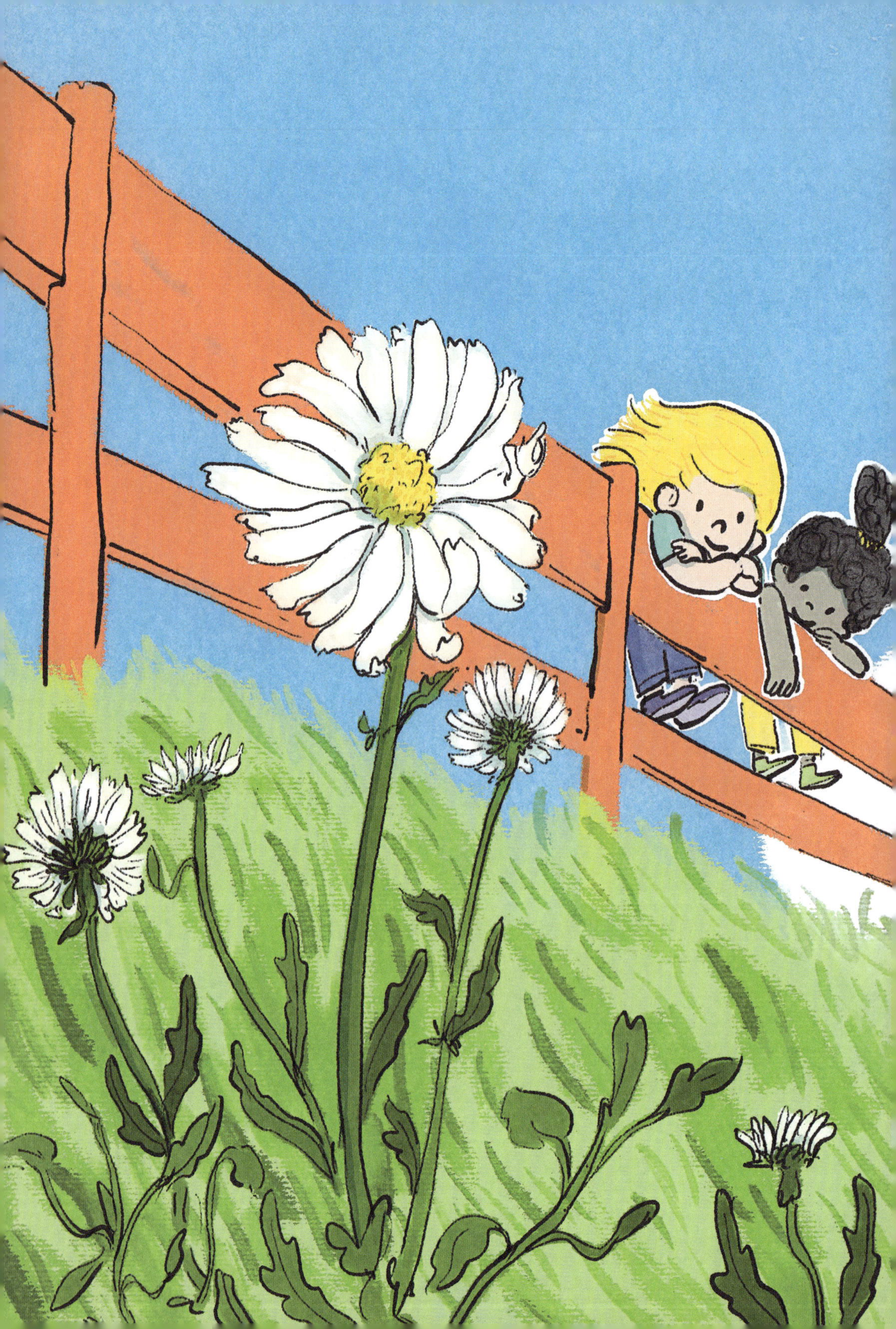

DAISY LIFE

A daisy lives a simple life,
A stranger to all stress and strife,
Happy to grow in park or field
And mingle with the farmer's yield.

By slow canals, by busy roads,
In tiny gardens, yet un-mowed,
By rivers wide or thin or forked,
A daisy watches all who walk.

A daisy lives a simple life,
A stranger to all stress and strife,
Flourishing wherever it grows,
Content to know what daisies know.

OLD BROWN BEAR

Old brown bear was an adventurer.
He climbed mountains, crossed rivers,
Catching fish with his bare paws.
His muscles rippled at the slightest threat:
He once fought a mountain lion,
Tore it like tissue paper and ate his fill.

But now he just sits at the bottom of my bed,
Next to Paddington, who has also seen better times.
They both prefer the days gone by,
When they were at the mercy of my narration,
When they were released into the wild
Imaginings of a boy with stories to tell.

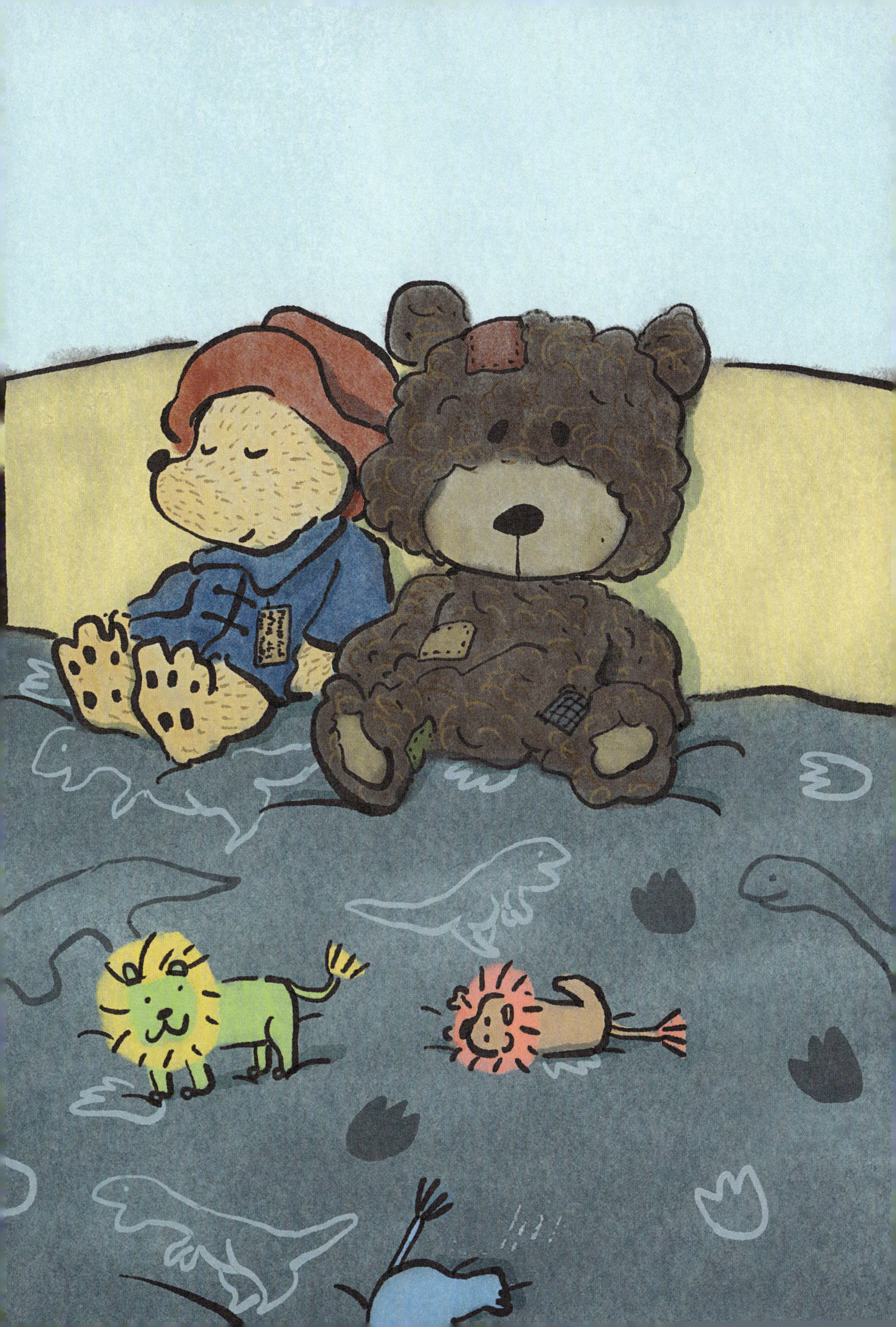

BRICK ON BRICK

Brick on brick.
Model finished
One more click
Reach the top
Don't give up
Brick on brick
Up and up
Higher, higher
Strong and thick
Making walls
Brick on brick
Push and snap
To the sky
Lego model
Building high
start here ⟶ Brick on brick

TATTERED

He strokes my cheek when I awake,
He holds my hand when it gets late,
And when I'm grumpy or unwell,
He has a calming, comfort smell.

    He's tattered, torn, with edges frayed,
    His fur is now a darker shade;
    But when my courage slips away,
    His threadbare love makes it okay.

SLED

until I'm at the top
and puff
and puff
and puff
and climb
and climb
and
I climb
with my sled

START HERE AND GO UP →

THEN
HERE
AND GO
DOWN → Then on my sled
          I whizz
              and whizz
                  and whizz
                      and slide
                          and slide
                              and slide
                                  so fast
                                    I cannot
                                       stop!

HELTER-SKELTER RIDE

You go whizzy, whizzy, whizzy,
And get very, very dizzy
On the helter-skelter slide.

You watch the clouds spin by
In the helter-skelter sky
On this curly, whirly, twisty, twirly ride.

You spiral down and down and down,
And race round and round and round
Until you feel all wobbly inside.

I'VE GOT A NEW BIKE

I've got a new bike,
I've got a new bike,
It's the one from the shop
That I said I would like.
It's got lots of gears,
The paint work is cool,
My friends crowd around
When I ride it to school.
It goes very fast,
It glides off the ground,
It silently breaks
The speed of sound.
My old one's gone
Down to the tip,
Dad said that I
Was too big for it.
So I've got a new bike,
I've got a new bike,
It's the one from the shop
That I said I would like.

UNICORN UNIFORM

I've got a unicorn pencil
And a unicorn pen,
I've got a unicorn cushion
In my unicorn den,

I wear a unicorn sticker
On my unicorn hand,
And I'd like to play horn
In a unicorn band,

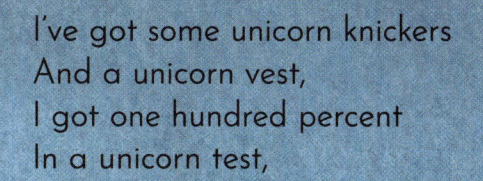

I've got some unicorn knickers
And a unicorn vest,
I got one hundred percent
In a unicorn test,

I've got a unicorn bottle
And a unicorn cup,
And I want to be a unicorn
When I grow up!

PLAYTIME SKIPPING

I skipped my happiness around
And as I skipped I quickly found
The noise increased upon the ground
As others skipped a happy sound.

Before too long our knees jerked high
And higher still, as we raced by,
With happy smiles and breathless sighs,
We were the sunshine in the sky.

Yet, when the whistle blew so shrill,
Our skipping legs hung straight and still,
Like soldiers in an army drill,
But happy hearts still skipped the thrill.

BRIGHT

When I was in year 2,
Head teacher said to me,
'Azad, when you grow up,
What would you like to be?'

He said, 'I have been told
That you are very bright,
So when you are grown up
How will you shine your light?'

So I thought hard and said:
'I'd love to be...a spark from a star,
The lightning flash from a racing car,
I'd love to be...the glow of the moon,
The flame from a rocket, making it zoom.
I'd love to be...the burn of the sun,
The glitter of glass as it sparkles and stuns.
I'd love to be...the flash from a fang
Of a Siberian tiger, chasing a man.
I'd love to be...a torch in a park
Where cats' eyes glow in the shadows of dark,
I'd love to be...the blaze of a fire,
And dance and dance, higher and higher.'

He looked at me, amazed,
And said, 'I meant a job,
Your answers don't match up,
Your answers are quite odd.

'You could be anything,
You could do what you love.'
I said, 'In that case, Sir,
My answers are above.'

BIG BOYS DON'T CRY

Big boys **do** cry -
When nobody's looking
Or the teacher's back is turned;
In the corner of the park,
When they get home,
(Under the duvet cover)

Big boys **do** cry -
Because words that sting
Can be flung so hard
That they can target
A big boy's heart,
And stab out the tears.

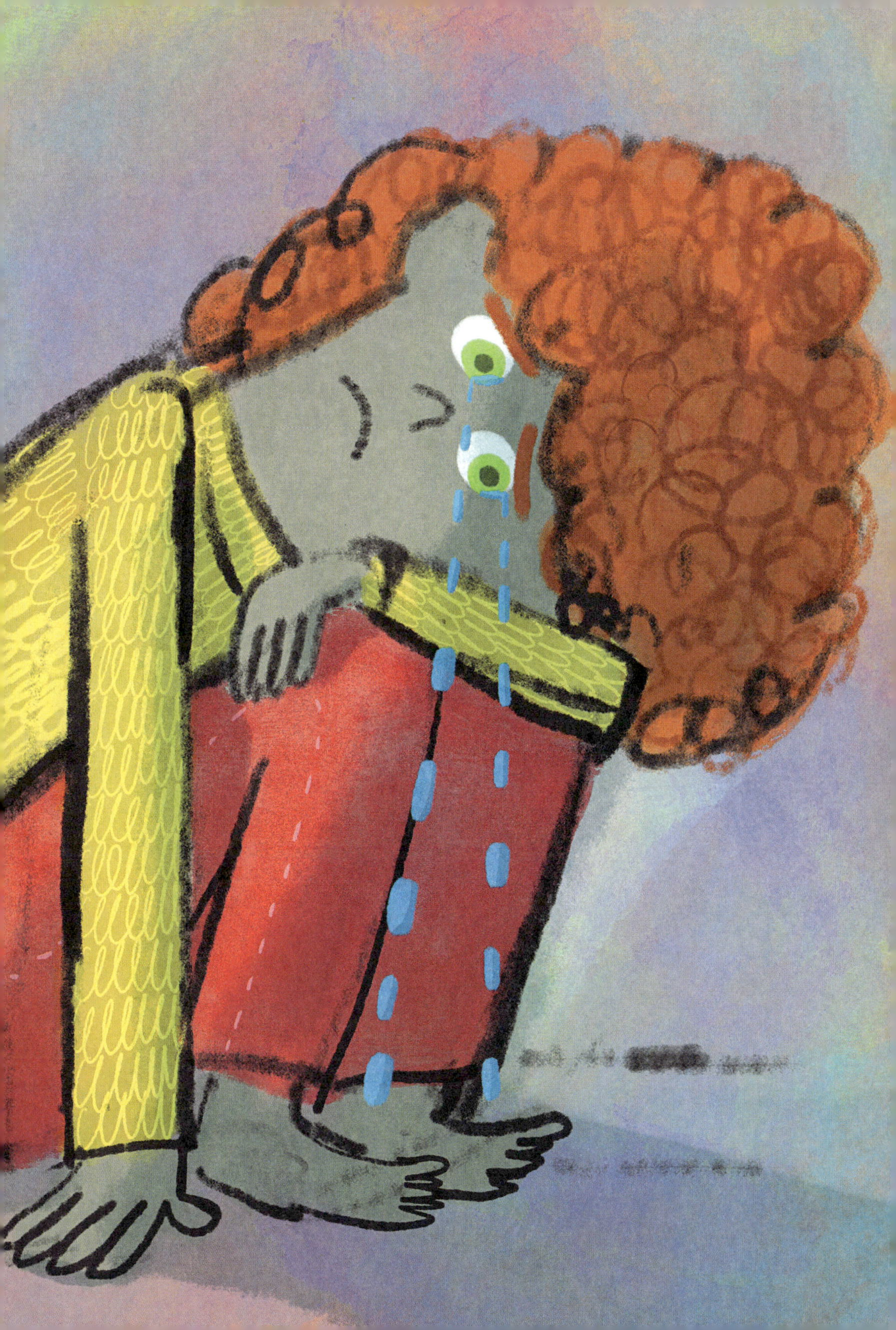

MUSTAFA'S JUMPER

Mustafa's jumper is alone in the hall,
It hangs from the bars fitted onto the wall.
The sleeve ends are frayed from Mustafa's nibbling,
When he thought very hard, was excitedly scribbling.

His stories were short, but each plot was real,
He told of long journeys, how sad people feel,
But over the weeks, his stories got longer,
The endings were happier, his smile got much stronger.

And Mustafa learnt the language we speak,
And all about book bags and days of the week.
Mustafa was moved to sit next to me,
And sometimes he came to my house for some tea.

Then, one day, Mustafa's mum knocked on the door,
She spoke to Miss Bennett, who stared at the floor,
Mustafa was leaving, the departure was soon,
And an icy anxiety flooded the room.

But it's Mustafa's jumper, it's Mustafa's chair,
It's Mustafa's workbook, and everyone cares
That Mustafa's gone to the airport today,
And right now, this minute, he's flying away.

So, I'll straighten his chair, and picture his face,
Pretend that he's scribbling his stories, with pace,
Then I'll rescue his jumper, and patch up the twine,
And hang it, with love, on the peg next to mine.

FRIDAY FEELING

At school you must be good
And never get there late,
But when it comes to Friday,
The children think it's great -

Because it's time for the weekend,
It's time to have a rest,
It's time to stay in bed 'til late
And walk round in your vest.

The teachers all work hard
To try to educate,
But when it comes to Friday,
The teachers think it's great -

Because it's time for the weekend,
It's time to have a rest,
It's time to stay in bed 'til late
And walk round in your vest.

The TAs work hard, too,
They help and motivate,
But when it comes to Friday,
The TAs think it's great -

Because it's time for the weekend,
It's time to have a rest,
It's time to stay in bed 'til late
And walk round in your vest.

CODE

The scientists say I'm written in code,
So I must be a mystery,
But when they've worked out my letters,
They'll notice they just spell out ME.

INVITATIONS

Lola is 6, she's wearing a sticker,
It's shiny and bright, the light makes its flicker,
And Macey and Daisy and Rufus and Marty
Are all going to go to Lola's 6th party.

Each invitation is sealed with a heart,
There's a sweetie inside, when you pull it apart,
And I wish and I wish I could go to her party
With Macey and Daisy and Rufus and Marty.

TING!
(YOU CAN PERFORM THIS WITH YOUR FRIENDS)

I'm waiting to ting
My triangle thing,
My friends nod along to the beat,
(*all nodding together*)

I'm waiting to ting
My triangle thing,
They're tapping their musical feet,
(*all tapping together*)

I'm waiting to ting
My triangle thing,
I turned up quite late to rehearse,
(*friends frown*)

I'm waiting to ting
My triangle thing,
Not now, at the end of the verse,
(*friend just stops him in time*)

I'm waiting to ting
My triangle thing,
The music gets louder and louder,

And that's when I ting
My triangle thing
And my friends just couldn't
be prouder! (*all clap*)

About the author

CORAL RUMBLE is one of our most popular poets: in 2018 she won the Caterpillar Poetry Prize. Having worked as a poet and performer for many years, she now specialises in writing and performing for children. *Riding a Lion*, published by Troika in 2020, was widely acclaimed and her most recent title, the verse novel *Little Light*, was published by Troika in 2021.

About the illustrator

SHIH-YU LIN was born in Taipei in Taiwan. He is a graduate of the MA illustration course at Cambridge School of Art. He now lives in London. His first book for Troika was *An Ordinary Story* published in 2019.